The Little Animal ABC Coloring Book

The Little
ANIMAL ABC
Coloring Book

Nina Barbaresi

DOVER PUBLICATIONS, INC.
New York

Bibliographical Note

The Little Animal ABC Coloring Book is a new work, first
published by Dover Publications, Inc., in 1988.

International Standard Book Number

ISBN-13: 978-0-486-25834-8
ISBN-10: 0-486-25834-3

Manufactured in the United States by LSC Communications
25834323   2020
www.doverpublications.com

Double your fun with the ABC's! Here are 26 delightful animals, one for each letter of the alphabet; each one is having fun doing an activity that begins with the same letter.

You've probably never seen a jaguar jumping rope, a baseball-playing bear or a parading panda, but these and 21 other funny animals fill the pages for you to color as you like. And don't forget to color in the letters too!

The Little Animal ABC Coloring Book

ARTISTIC ALLIGATOR

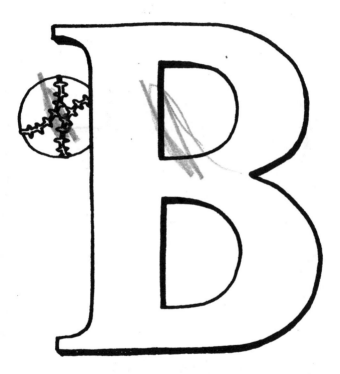

BATTING BEAR

CLOWNING CAT

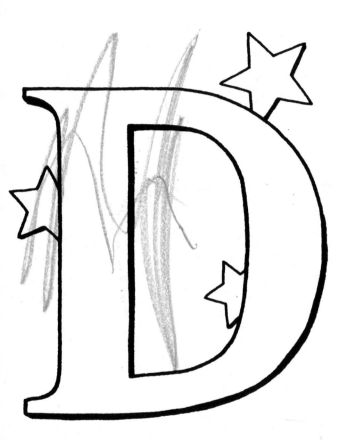

DANCING DUCK

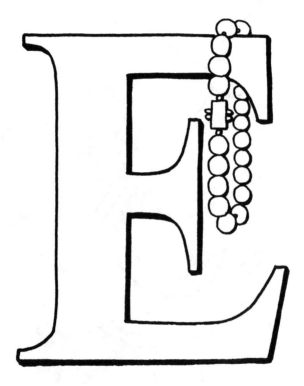

ELEGANT ELEPHANT

FREEZING FROG

GULPING GORILLA

HUNGRY HIPPO

INTERESTED INSECT

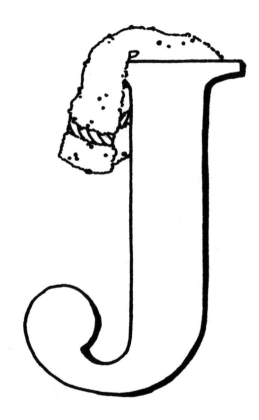

JUMPING JAGUAR

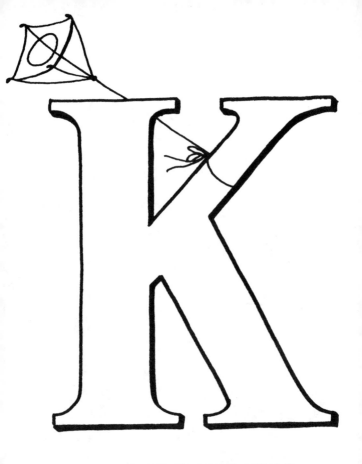

KICKING KANGAROO

LAZY LION

MARRYING MOUSE

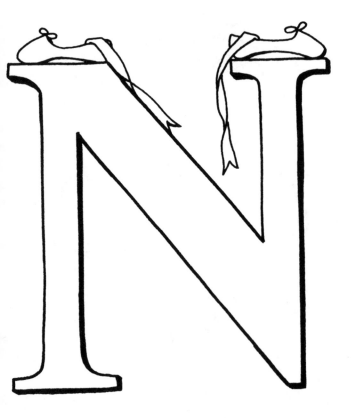

NIMBLE NEWT

ORDERLY OWL

PARADING PANDA

41

QUESTIONING QUAIL

RUNNING RABBIT

SAVING SQUIRREL

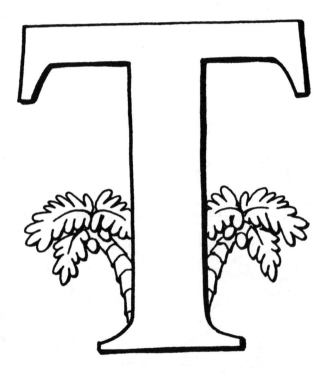

TRAVELING TURTLE

UNIFORMED UNICORN

VAIN VICUÑA

53

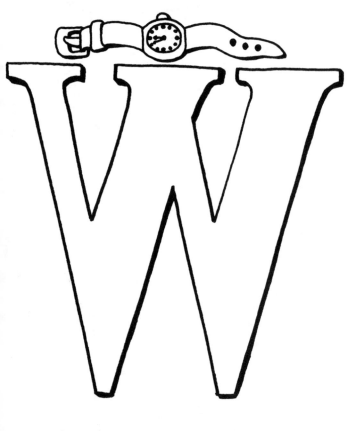

WAITING WOODCHUCK

X-RAYED XIPHIAS*

*Another name for Swordfish.

YAWNING YAK

ZANY ZEBRA